T0042553

# Blue Mountain Ballads

Words by
## TENNESSEE WILLIAMS
Music by
## PAUL BOWLES

## CONTENTS

Cover Photo:
Kosti Ruohomaa (Black Star)

ED-3204

ISBN 978-0-7935-5104-0

## G. SCHIRMER, Inc.

DISTRIBUTED BY
HAL•LEONARD®
CORPORATION
7777 W. BLUEMOUND RD. P.O. BOX 13819 MILWAUKEE, WI 53213

Copyright © 1979 by G. Schirmer, Inc. (ASCAP) New York, NY
International Copyright Secured. All Rights Reserved.
**Warning:** Unauthorized reproduction of this publication is
prohibited by Federal law and subject to criminal prosecution.

# Heavenly Grass

Tennessee Williams

Paul Bowles

Copyright, 1946, by G. Schirmer, Inc.
International Copyright Secured
Printed in the U. S. A.

48130c

4

feet took a walk    In heav-en-ly grass.    All    night while the lone - some

stars    rolled    past,    Then my feet come down    to    walk    on earth    And my

moth - er cried When she    give    me    birth.

# Lonesome Man

Tennessee Williams

Paul Bowles

Copyright, 1946, by G. Schirmer, Inc.
International Copyright Secured
Printed in the U. S. A.

way. My_ teef chaw - chaw on an old ham bone an' I

do the dish - es all a - lone,

I do the dish - es all_ by my lone. My

feet clop - clop    on the    hard - wood floor 'cause I    won't buy love    at the

hard - ware store,    I    don't want love    from the    mer - can - tile    store.

Now the    clock tick - tocks    by my

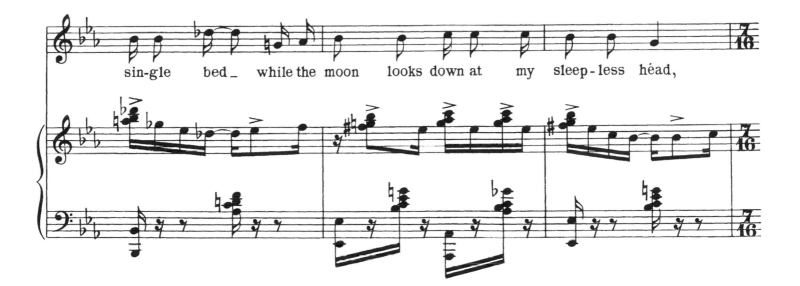

sin-gle bed — while the moon looks down at my sleep-less head,

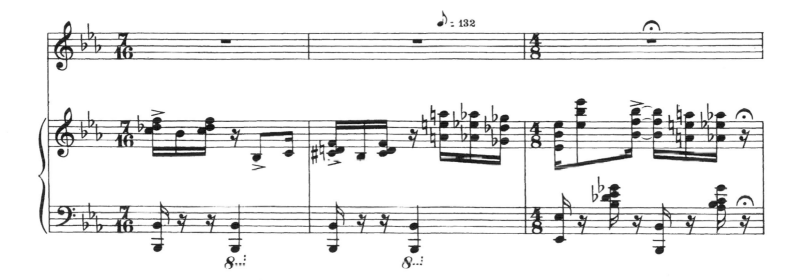

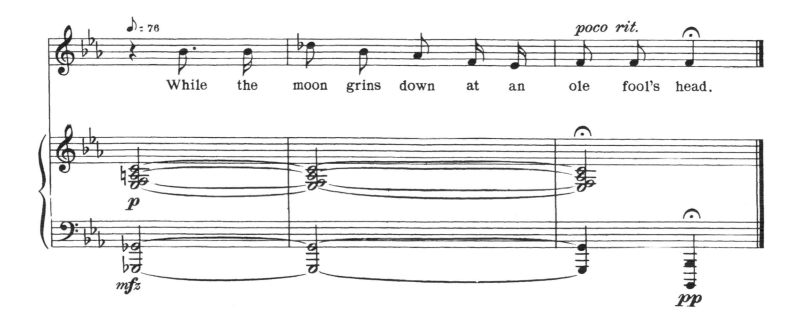

While the moon grins down at an ole fool's head.

# Cabin

Tennessee Williams

Paul Bowles

Copyright, 1946, by G. Schirmer, Inc.
International Copyright Secured
Printed in the U. S. A.

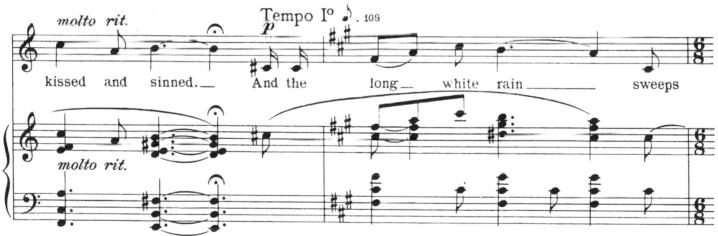

# Sugar in the Cane

Tennessee Williams

Paul Bowles

Copyright, 1946, by G. Schirmer, Inc.
International Copyright Secured
Printed in the U. S. A.

Nev - er touched ex-cept by rain. ___ If you touched me God save you, These

sum-mer days are hot and blue. ___

I'm po-ta-toes not yet mashed,

I'm a check that ain't been cashed.__ I'm a win-dow with a blind,

Can't see what goes on be - hind.__ If you did, God save your soul! These

win - ter nights are blue and cold!_____

ten.